Higher Ground

Original Art and Photo Credit by Shirley A. Genovese © 2019
All Rights Reserved

As sailors look for the lighthouse to guide them safely to land, they have a confident expectation that the light will shine bright and steady to lead them to their destination. Jesus is the light that leads me to higher ground. He is the Life-Light that blazed out of the darkness; and the darkness cannot stop it. (John 1)

A CONFIDENT EXPECTATION
40 Hope-Full Conversations

By Shirley A. Genovese

A Confident Expectation 40 Hope-Full Conversations
By Shirley A. Genovese
First Edition
Copyright © 2019 by Shirley A. Genovese

ISBN: 978-1-733174008 Printed
ISBN: 978-1-733174015 eBook

~Dedication and Acknowledgements~

For Charles, my husband and dearest friend. I wake up filled with the joy of life together. Our home is a place of trust where love abounds, wrapped in humor. It is a perfect place to pursue a dream. I love being your wife. You have my heart forever. This book could not have happened without you.

To my publishing mentors: Uta Milewski and Lisa Varco. Thank you for living lives that show case your love for others. Your generous sharing of publishing intricacies is the reason this book is not just a dream. I admire you, as I do your books. You have shown me the way with great grace. Thank you.

To my friend Edith Housel: Thank you for your editing support and for encouraging me on this adventure.

To my friend Reverend Michael Wing: My perspective shifted as you taught the Word of God. It allowed the seeds of a dream to flourish and become this book. Thank you for showing me how to adjust my vision to see what is possible with faith in Jesus Christ. It gave me hope.

To my friend Terri Ackerman: Do you remember challenging me to examine my beliefs during a difficult time when despair was trying to take hold? I did. God is faithful. I have hope today of which this book testifies. Thank you, dear friend.

To my family and friends: You have prayed me through to the end. Your love and encouragement surround me. I can walk new paths with you by my side. Love is a powerful force. Thank you for your expressions of love and companionship. Life is rich.

Table of Contents

~Foreword~

A caterpillar transforms in the darkness of its cocoon and comes into the light a new beautiful creature. A similar journey by the author birthed the words of this book. Shirley Genovese has gone into the cocoon of God's presence and emerged transformed. In *A Confident Expectation*, we all get to enjoy the beautiful transformation that has resulted.

Reverend Michael D. Wing
Lead Pastor
Lockport Christian Church

I remember the first day I met Shirley Genovese. We were sitting at the same table at a church conference and she had just received a physical healing. That was over ten years ago and I have watched her blossom in her creative expression of the Lord's love. She has a unique ability to bring out God's watchful, loving care into the everyday activities of life. Her writing style brings the reader comfort and encouragement to press on no matter what life circumstances bring. I am honored to call Shirley my intercessor, my friend.

Terri Ackerman
Care Pastor
Lockport Christian Church

~Preface~

The Light is always shining through the trees. A slight shift in our vision allows us to see it from a different vantage point. We catch the brilliance of a new perspective. It makes a way for change. I hope you do not rush through this book. I hope you linger on the conversations, enjoy His presence, and savor the time. I hope you talk with God and listen to His love lessons. Let Hope arise.

~Introduction~

I believe that God is always speaking because He loves us and wants us to know Him. It is a matter of learning to discern His voice among the others. It is the fruit of asking Him to make Himself known in new ways and to open our hearts to discern more when He speaks. I want to have a deeper understanding and confidence in Him. I have a desire for the treasures of His heart, which He has prepared for me, because I love Him. So, I ask Him. *A Confident Expectation* expresses my hope that it will lead you to unshakeable faith. Each page is a testament of God's love and faithfulness. He waits for us to listen when He speaks. I hope you find this to be true as you join me and step into a life that is alive with promise.

Consider This: Conversations in *A Confident Expectation* are my own conclusions born out of my relationship with Jesus Christ. I offer them for thought-provoking consideration. Everyone must come to their own conclusions and decide their own responses. My conversations included in this book are not advice. I offer *A Confident Expectation* to encourage you as you seek a deeper understanding and relationship with God. He wants us to know Him so He can turn our coal into diamonds and our ore into gold, if we let Him. May hope grow in you. This is my prayer for you.

Your Thoughts? Here is where I invite you to record your own conversations with God and His responses. Write often. Write well.

Bible References: I included the book of the Bible and Chapter without the specific verse because a verse in context to its place in the Bible can clarify and provide insight other than what I have included in this book. I *italicized* all verses I quoted. In some places where there is no quoted verse, I have also included book and chapter for further study reference.

1~   Let Light Shine Through

Last weekend, my husband and I took a leisurely walk through a nearby park, enjoying a picnic lunch as our reward. It is a beautiful place in the middle of a large suburb. When we are in the park, we cannot hear the traffic. You can convince yourself you are in the middle of a forest preserve. It is serene; filled with old-growth trees, new growth, animals and sunlight filtering through the rich leaf cover. It is a restorative place. There are sunny and shady areas to walk through. As we rested on a bench, I could see only a little sun twinkling through the denseness of the treetops. As I raised my camera to capture the moment, I realized I had to shift my position and my camera to where I could see the ball of fire blazing through between the leaves.

Consider This: As I looked at the photo later, with that bright ball of light and sun rays blazing through the dark leaf canopy, I realized it was an earthly reminder of our life with God. We wonder where God is. Our spiritual eyesight and heart beats are trying to reach God but stuff is in the way. We may need to shift our vision, thoughts and emotions just enough to see the bright Glory of the Son, who is always with us; loving and lighting our path with His wisdom. I write, hoping our vision becomes clearer and we will be certain of His presence even in dark places.

"What came into existence was Life, and the Life was the Light to live by. The Life-Light blazed out of the darkness; the darkness could not put it out." John 1:5 (MSG).

Your Thoughts?

_____

_____

§

2~ Blessed: Inside the Best Love Ever

A godly man wrote in a letter to a young pastor, *"All scripture is inspired by God and is useful for teaching, rebuking, correcting and training in righteousness."* But that was after the apostle Paul had written in the same letter, *"You (Timothy)... know all about my teaching, my way of life, my purpose, faith, patience, love, endurance, persecutions and sufferings. Yet the Lord rescued me from them all."* (2 Timothy 3).

<u>Consider This:</u> When Timothy read his letters from Paul, he knew that they were the real deal. He knew he could trust the advice, instruction, encouragement, and everything Paul said because Timothy knew the author. This is how Paul appealed to him; as one man in relationship with another. Paul was saying, 'Do not just take my word for it. You know me. You have been with me as I suffered many things and you saw how I reacted when faced with hardship. I was just as steadfast in the good times as I was in the hard times. You know my heart and how I stayed the course. Timothy, you know God is real. You have seen how He has kept me in difficult times.' Timothy must have read Paul's letters over and over, learning from one who had run the course well.

When I read my Bible today, I read it as one knowing the Author. I am not saying this with arrogance. Our relationship has developed. His patience has made the difference in my deepening understanding of His nature. I think about His heart motivation for inspiring whatever scripture I happen to be reading. I look beyond sets of rules and religious practices to how the truth applies today. I look to the life of Jesus on earth and all I have learned about God's nature through Him. In the Bible, these lessons start in Genesis and end in Revelation. When I wake up every morning, the lessons continue as I find Him waiting. He speaks fresh words each day. His words are in my heart because of my relationship with Him. When I open my Bible, the verses come alive to me like no other book ever written.

If I did not know the Author of this marvelous book, the Bible, I might read it as any other without gleaning the life changing truths in it.

5

I might find it dry and boring, without relevance. This is what I did before I knew God's love in Jesus and began to understand His love story with us. Inspired by God as He breathed on men to write, it instructs and encourages me. An acronym that best describes the Bible: Blessed Inside Best Love Ever.

Your thoughts?

_____

_____

_____

_____

_____

_____

_____

_____

_____

_____

_____

_____§

3~ Felling Giants

He was a shepherd, poet, warrior, king, and prophet in his life-time. His family thought little of him compared to his older brothers. They may have thought him a dreamer only worthy to watch the sheep. Yet, David was the one who faced and killed Goliath when the whole army of Israel feared to engage with him. David trusted in God to deliver. The shepherd had become a warrior. He was fresh from the hills and caring for the flock. Where did his skill and courage to confront giants begin? Where did he learn the power of words to ease pain, lift the spirit of man and to ask God for skillful strength?

Consider This: David's job as a youth had been tending his father's sheep; alert for danger while the sheep were grazing in the sun or in their enclosure at night. He called on God for deliverance from predators. In his shepherd years, David learned the power of God's words. He relied on the Lord for the skill and courage to kill the lion and the bear. He learned to dance before the Lord and worship Him with song. One day he brought provision to his brothers battling the Philistines. That was the day he killed a giant and saved Israel.

As David did, we can learn the attributes of inner strength and the skill of enduring in the quiet or hard places in life where our Father in heaven sees us. God comes beside us to help and cheer us forward because He desires our success as a spiritual people. He loves to speak and show us His heart, character, and personality; gathering us into His purposes. During these quieter times, He is preparing us for future mighty deeds of faith. This gives me hope. David was far from a perfect man who lived a life full of highs and lows. Yet, he never blamed God for the difficulties and sorrows in his life. He never stopped worshipping God with the songs of his heart.

Alone on our hills today we can be strong in the might of the Lord. We have giants to slay and dances awaiting us. Sing your own song to Him! Select the perfect words for battle as stones for the sling-shot! Dance before Him on injustice and with great joy! Rest in Him with a confident expectation and watch for the amazing to happen. Let God arise and His enemies be scattered!

Your Thoughts?

_____

_____

_____

_____

_____

_____

_____

_____

_____

_____

_____

_____

_____

_____

_____ §

4~   While Bethlehem Sleeps

Foretold thousands of years before its fulfillment, the promise of Christ's conception and birth came when Ephraim attacked Jerusalem. God in His great compassion gave a message of hope that a virgin would conceive and give birth to a son and His name would be Immanuel, which means *"God is with us."* (Isaiah 7). No matter what happens, God promises His presence. Fast forward to the time of Matthew, who reminded everyone the sign of the Redeemer was the virgin birth. A divine mystery and miracle. Immanuel was to have other names. Names infused with promise and power. Wonderful Counselor, Mighty God, Prince of Peace, the Son of the Highest, Messiah, Savior, Jesus; to name just a few. As the prophet Micah foretold, this extraordinary birth took place in Bethlehem (Micah 5). Jesus was born into a community who learned the prophecies of Isaiah and Micah from an early age, along with the other stories of their ancestors. Even so, the significance of this event went unnoticed by many; as people slept the night He was born.

Consider This: It was not an accident of birth that the Redeemer was born in Bethlehem (Ephraim's former land). Or that Caesar decreed a census for people to register in their ancestral towns just at the time Mary was to give birth. It was not a coincidence that shepherds were out in the fields keeping watch over their flocks at night. Or that a guest room was not available to the parents and wise men saw a star in the sky. It happened by the mighty hand of God. He kept His promise and more, even as people slept. Yet a small band of people paid attention: the humble parents heard, the shepherds watched and the wise men looked. They saw it unfold, believed, sought the promised Child, and worshipped Him.

When John the Baptist asked if Jesus was who they were waiting for or should they expect another, Jesus replied that the blind saw, the deaf heard, the lame walked, the sick were no longer ill, the dead lived and the poor heard the Good News (Matthew 11). Each of us must come to our own conclusion about this amazing Child, whose birth filled the skies with the glory of the Lord and hosts of angels. He has given us new birth into a living hope (1 Peter 1).

9

"Do not be afraid. I bring you good news that will cause great joy for all people. Today in the town of David, a Savior is born to you; He is the Messiah, the Lord." (Luke 2).

Your Thoughts?

_____

_____

_____

_____

_____

_____

_____

_____

_____

_____

_____

_____

_____ §

5~ What is New?

The coming of a new year causes us to hope for something different. We raise prayers for a new thing from the Lord. We seek fresh words from the Holy Spirit. It is good to be alert and watchful when we do and to remember Adam and Eve. They had an intimate relationship with God. He lavished His best of creation on them in love. He gave them purpose and looked for them to talk over the day and enjoy their company. Yet they believed a subtle lie about God. Adam and Eve believed the serpent more than God with whom they had an intimate relationship. It may have been because the serpent appealed to something hidden in the depths of their hearts, something they desired more than God. This is a cautionary tale for us.

People will say they have heard special words from the Holy Spirit describing God's plans for us, for nations and many other topics. Many will accept every word as coming from God. It can be seductive. It is good to remember that we are not stronger than Adam and Eve.

Consider This: I believe that God still speaks to our hearts by the Holy Spirit and the Bible; words that align with the other words in the Bible because He does not contradict Himself. He does not lead us with confusion. Scripture tells us not to disregard every prophecy because some might be false or quench the Spirit; treating true prophecies with contempt. We need to test the message and hold on to what is true and reject the false (1 Thessalonians 5) while discerning the motivation of the prophets (1 John 4). Reliable prophetic words come from men and women who speak from God through the Holy Spirit, not by the will of man (2 Peter 1).

How can we discern the false? We wait for it to come to pass. People in bible times asked the question. *"How can we know when a message has not been spoken by the Lord?"* The answer came as, *"If what a prophet proclaims in the name of the Lord does not take place or come true, that is a message the Lord has not spoken."* (Deuteronomy 18). It is gracious of God to explain.

The Lord is faithful to His word. We can rest in Him. My prayer is that you receive everything that God in His great love has already made available to you. Hope is a powerful thing when we know the source of our hope is trustworthy. Who is the source of your hope?

Your Thoughts?

_____

_____

_____

_____

_____

_____

_____

_____

_____

_____

_____

_____§

6~   Resurrection Redemption

Bereft by the empty tomb, Mary Magdalene went to tell the disciples who did not believe her. Simon Peter went right into the empty tomb but still did not understand what had happened. Mary lingered there. Peter returned to the disciples bewildered and afraid (John 20). When Jesus visited the disciples and showed them His hands and feet, they believed what they saw. Except Thomas, who was not there. When he heard what had happened, he greeted the wonderful news with unbelief. He required proof, too. A week later, the disciples including Thomas, were again behind locked doors. Jesus came to visit and invited Thomas to touch the nail holes in His hands and the sword hole in his side. Thomas believed. When Jesus appeared on the shore of Galilee, the disciples again did not recognize Him until He performed the miracle of the fish-filled net. The men on the road to Emmaus thought He was a stranger because He asked them questions about recent events. They talked about the crucifixions. They recognized Him during supper when Jesus broke the bread and gave it to them.

Consider This: Despite all that Jesus had told people, they did not understand. When it happened as Jesus said, they did not recognize Him at first. Until He did something for each of them.

With Mary, He called her name. With Thomas, He gave him irrefutable evidence. He greeted Peter and other disciples in a way that encouraged the weary fishermen. He made them breakfast. To the men on the way to Emmaus He was patient as He re-explained God's plan for salvation. Jesus knows what will bring each person to the place of recognizing who He is and to fullness of faith in Him. He is patient and personal as He leads each of us to faith. What is your story? What do you need to believe in Him?

We struggle when we do not understand. All of us need someone to walk with us on the road to faith. When I understood that I could ask Him to show Himself to me, I did. He came. This is the day the adventure began. Anyone can ask. I hope you do.

13

Your Thoughts?

_____

_____

_____

_____

_____

_____

_____

_____

_____

_____

_____

_____

_____

_____

_____

_____§

7~ Ascension Affirmation

Jesus approached the eleven disciples several times after His resurrection to discuss their fears and strengthen their faith in Him. Each time He had something important to say and instruction to give them. Why was it so hard for them to believe it was Him? In Luke 24, it shows them in great stress and emotional. They...

- Became startled and frightened, thinking they saw a ghost.
- Did not believe it because of joy and amazement. It was too good to be true.
- Did not understand the truths He taught them. It was confusing.

Dashed expectations and intense human emotions clouded their thinking. It was just plain hard to believe. They did not realize that the love, time and teaching He poured into them was preparing them for their greatest purpose, which was to take Jesus to the world. It was unfathomable. How were they to do this without Him and why did He care so much that they believed He had risen from the dead and understood His teachings? Because the task He was giving them was so immense and impossible, that unless they believed He was the Savior, they would fail. *"You are eyewitnesses of these things,"* He told them. The disciples had no way of knowing we would seek, listen, learn, and believe today.

Consider This: We do not always understand how scriptures apply to our lives or connect what the Bible says to our circumstances. We do not always recognize that Jesus is with us through them and can become overwhelmed. We cannot always see the bigger picture because we become immersed in the present, or the past, and cannot yet see the future or our place in it.

Jesus Christ is our hope. We have spiritual power and authority available in the Holy Spirit. We have a Father in heaven who loves us with never-ending love. When we are sure of who He is, we can gather our courage to do the things He calls us to do, regardless of our circumstances. He loves to take weak things and show Himself strong on our behalf. He loves us. We have a divine purpose. He is near to us. He is preparing our launch to the next thing He has for us. Small or large, His plans for us are good. The last thing heard from the angel after Jesus' ascension was 'He will come back!' Good news for us. While we are waiting, let us be ready for the new thing He wants to do in us, for us and through us.

Your Thoughts?

_____

_____

_____

_____

_____

_____

_____

_____

_____

_____

_____

_____§

8~ Wait Where?

After His resurrection, Jesus told his followers to wait for him in Jerusalem. They must have felt leaderless, anxious, isolated, grieving, directionless, abandoned, and perplexed. They had received so many exciting promises from Jesus, then they were told to wait. He said he had a plan. They wanted to be doing things. But He said he would not leave them alone. There was much more to say to them. He said that they grieved while the world rejoiced but that their grief would turn into joy. They trusted him and waited.

Flashback with me to a place called Kadesh, which was the chief waiting place of the Israelites before they entered the promised land; the land that is now Israel. It was just on the southern edge of Canaan. They may have waited there for years in sight of their destination. The region was hot, dry, desolate and without rain. Fed by streams draining from the Negev in the spring, it was desert. And it was holy. How could this inhospitable place be holy?

Consider This: I will admit that I do not wait patiently. The question is not why, but how will I wait. Will I...

- calm my restlessness in His presence and receive respite from my emotions? (Psalm 62)
- honor Him while I wait, protecting my heart and mind? (Philippians 4)
- encourage myself in His promises? (2 Peter 1)
- weep in pain and despair to receive His comfort and strength? (1 Samuel 30)
- ask Him how long (Psalm 119) and listen for His words? (Psalm 85)
- remember the streams in the desert places? (Isaiah 35)
- wait expectantly and eagerly? (Micah 7)

Psalm 29 is amazing in the waiting. There is One who knows where I am. He has sent the gift of the Holy Spirit to be with me as I wait. Will I remember *"The voice of the Lord shakes the desert; the Lord shakes the Desert of Kadesh?"* Yes, I will remember His power to quiet me, set my feet on a firm foundation and, in time, deliver me. He makes all things new. I will learn how infinite, unfailing, and tender His love is toward me, His beloved. I will learn to trust Him in all things. And when I cannot, when I can only cry "Jesus", I will! He will come to me. I will wait until the waiting is over, transformed in the waiting with Him. It is then I will realize the desert has transformed into a Holy place.

Your Thoughts?

_____

_____

_____

_____

_____

_____

_____

_____

_____

_____

_____

_____§

9~   Who Do You Say I Am?

They were a small group standing on a hill gazing into the sky. They had just watched their closest companion, best loved friend and hope for Israel leave them. We can only imagine what they were thinking and feeling. The angels nudged them from their reverie to remind them it was not the end. With this hope, they roused themselves to walk back to Jerusalem to the upper room, where they were staying (Matthew 17). Between the time Jesus ascended and the beginning of Pentecost, a huge shift occurred within these men. One minute they were standing with Jesus asking Him questions, ever the students. The next time we hear from Peter, he is leading the others with authority and confidence for a decision. These men became apostles that day and stepped into their life purpose. They had realized who they were born to be in Christ. It was a powerful awakening. It was to shake Jerusalem and the ends of the earth. Their response? They spent the next ten days in prayer; waiting.

Consider This: Beforehand, Peter had publicly denied his identity in Jesus three times (John 18). It was the forgiving love of Christ that awakened Peter to his purpose. Peter grieved that Jesus asked him three times if he loved Him, until he realized that Jesus had forgiven him for each incident of denial. It was a loving act of affirmation of who Peter was in Jesus' eyes. If someone had asked Peter who he was just before Jesus ascended, he might have replied he was a disciple of Jesus; afterward an apostle. Jesus acknowledged Peter's weaknesses with loving forgiveness and affirmed His purpose for Peter's life as being the rock on which "*I will build my church.*" (Matthew 16). Peter finally understood. He moved full steam into this new life for which he was born.

We can see ourselves with cloudy vision, just as Peter did. We think others are more; more gifted, anointed, relationally adept, qualified to speak, unafraid and bolder, or whatever we are not. We long to know what God thinks of us, who He sees us to be and who we are in Him. Peter needed to know who he was in the eyes of Jesus. We do too.

We have a purpose. Understanding that purpose begins and ends with the conversations we have with Him. It will be a powerful awakening! I am excited, are you?

Your Thoughts?

_____

_____

_____

_____

_____

_____

_____

_____

_____

_____

_____

_____

_____

_____§

10~ You Want Me to Do What?

Have you ever wondered what the newly minted apostles were thinking and feeling as the enormity of their first assignment settled on them? Their brief resume might look like this:

Professional Objectives: To create an apostolic ministry in all nations. To baptize them in the name of the Father, the Son, and the Holy Spirit. Teach new believers. Will travel.

Education:
- Standard Temple education
- Fisherman, tax collectors and similar occupations.
- Discipled by Jesus, son of Joseph, also known as the Son of God.
- Completed ministry internship.

Strengths:
- Generating Income through tax collecting
- Fishing
- Crowd management
- Faithfulness

Areas for Development Potential:
- Sleep Management: stay awake to pray
- Dependability: support friends in their hour of need
- Comprehension of new spiritual truths

This is an exaggeration but I wonder if they felt unqualified for the task given to them. Little did they know that when Jesus called out to them 'Follow me!' it would lead to this. What were they to do? They prayed! For ten days until the Gift came!

Consider This: Many of us face assignments which require more than we know how to do. Is it the same for you? Surely, even in their exhaustion from the gut-wrenching events that had taken place recently, they remembered: *"Come to me, all you who are weary and burdened,*

21

and I will give you rest." (Matthew 11). The empowering Holy Spirit led them as they followed the path laid out. What will we do with the life changing opportunities the Holy Spirit will present to us? And at the end, will we say *"You have shown me the way of life, granted me the joy of Your presence and the pleasures of living with You forever?"* (Psalm 16). Excuse me now, as I need to have a conversation with my Father in heaven and remember my lessons. I will see you on the road and we can share our stories and rejoice together.

Your Thoughts?

_____

_____

_____

_____

_____

_____

_____

_____

_____

_____

_____

_____§

11~ Listening for the Holy

They were still in the upper room the morning the Gift came suddenly; with an amazing display of the Holy. A violent wind came from heaven and filled the whole house. Can you picture it? I believe the holiness of their waiting and the extended time of prayer after the sorrow, fear, and confusion fostered the spiritual climate to usher in this deeper immersion into God. The apostles were at the end of themselves, had done everything that Jesus had told them to do and were ready for God to move.

Consider This: The description of a violent wind reminds me of the strong winds parting the Red Sea, after Noah's flood to dry up the waters and when the quail entrée came on the wind. These were stormy winds that did His bidding referred to in Psalm 148. These winds brought rescue, new life and provision in a way never experienced by God's people (Genesis 8, Exodus 14, Numbers 11). For Elijah, one great period of life had just ended. Exhausted he could not see the future. The Lord told him to stand in a sheltered part of a mountain. The Lord passed by. A great and powerful wind tore the mountains apart. Then an earthquake came followed by fire. The wind was so strong it rearranged the face of the mountain. When Elijah heard it end in a whisper he moved to stand at the mouth of the cave. This is where the Lord tells him He has provided a new focus for Elijah; a young prophet named Elisha whose name means 'God is Salvation.' He heard holiness in the whisper. He came out before the Lord, stilling his soul long enough to listen. The demonstration of God's keeping power in the storm had to come first so he could hear the gentle whisper.

God does not always remove the obstacles, pain, and desert from our lives right away. In these examples, the strong wind brought something necessary and extraordinary. It ushered in new powerful beginnings and His power to carry out new missions. It cleansed the house, swept away the staleness and brought renewed energy and focus for the new to begin. I can become so focused on the storms and desert I do most of the talking sometimes. He sees me, knows me, and loves me in it. When I remember, I can quiet myself to hear the gentle whispers from His heart.

23

The freshening comes, and He speaks newness; instills a new level of power and authority for the new thing that is coming. Because of the storms, I can hear the Holy.

Your Thoughts?

_____

_____

_____

_____

_____

_____

_____

_____

_____

_____

_____

_____

_____§

12~ Promise in the Fire

There they were, the Jesus followers, praying for ten days in the second floor of a rented house in Jerusalem. Have you ever prayed for ten days straight with no interruptions except for a meal now and then? Ten days seeking the Lord. They would have been progressively entering a deeper place with God. They were waiting for the promised Holy Spirit. It was a new experience. I do not know if the fire and wind that came with the Holy Spirit surprised them. The scriptures they had learned from childhood had many references to wind and fire. These men and women knew fire well. They knew God was in the fire of acceptance that burned up the required sacrifices for the forgiveness of sins and in the purifying refiner's fire of Malachi 3. They knew God in the attention-getting burning bush that Moses encountered which changed the course of his life and brought him face to face with his divine purpose. They knew God in the pillar of fire at night that protected them and the fire of God's consecration that marked Solomon's Temple as God's place. They knew that fire was a sign of God's presence in the house that day. They knew that the long-awaited Holy Spirit had arrived. They stopped praying and started to praise and glorify God (Acts 2).

Consider This: Forest and wild fires, while devastating, allow for new growth and rebuilding. Seeds of the trees and plants, scattered before a fire, lay dormant for years for such a time. After a fire, the seeds respond to the fire's intense heat by bursting open and letting the life inside get loose. The ashes feed the soil so that the freed life can take hold and prosper with renewed nutrient rich soil. It is a God ordained regeneration process.

The fire times are when I wonder where God is, the One who says He loves me and will never leave me or forsake me. It is easy to lose my way. He is my only Hope. I seek His sustaining presence. I pray, not holding back anything. Sometimes, I can say nothing. I know that God never leaves me. I begin to understand that He accepts me, gets my attention, purifies my desires, and changes the course of my life. He brings me a greater understanding of my divine purpose. I am a fertile place where new life can grow. The seeds He planted over the years found a place to grow in the spiritual riches that remained. I am better prepared for my mission, It took me a while to see this. He was patient. *"The Lord has done this. It is marvelous in our eyes."* (Mark 10).

Your Thoughts?

_____

_____

_____

_____

_____

_____

_____

_____

_____

_____

_____

_____

_____§

13~ The Story Heard Around the World

The room exploded with spontaneous worship. It was not an ordinary quiet affair. The promised gift of the Holy Spirit had arrived. Immersed in His presence, they were praising and declaring the mighty wonders of God in languages and dialects unknown by the speakers. Some people thought they were drunk. The God-fearing Jews, in Jerusalem for Pentecost, heard it. Crowded Jerusalem had swelled to four or five times above the normal population. People traveled far; from Rome, Libya, what is now Iran, Iraq, Turkey, and the Roman Empire. They heard the praises of God, in their own languages and dialects, from uneducated, untraveled Galileans. Peter, freshly filled with the Holy Spirit, stood up and told his story with the inner power, authority, and boldness of the Holy Spirit (Acts 2). Three thousand confessed faith in Jesus that day, with the numbers increasing daily. It happened as He said. From prayer to praise to telling their story, these eye witnesses saw God establish His church in Jerusalem first. As with everyone who arrives home from a trip, the visitors to Jerusalem told their stories of this event. In doing so, they unwittingly planted seeds for the church to grow to the uttermost parts of the world.

Consider This: It started when a handful of people heard Jesus say to them 'Follow Me' and they did. Since that day, their lives had been full of new adventures, huge challenges, joys, and sorrows; each bringing a deeper understanding of the plans of God for their lives. Without their faithfulness in telling their eyewitness stories of the things Jesus said and did, we would not hear it today. Their story was the story of Jesus who came to show us the face and heart of God. They knew they had an amazing true story they could not resist telling.

Jesus' ministry was one of telling stories about His Father's love for people and hearts far from God. He urged people to draw near with faith to the best thing that could happen to them. He had a story to tell; which He did. All of us have stories. I love a good story. Especially stories of how faith in Jesus has blossomed. Life is richer for stories. They help us make connections with others. We learn we are not alone.

27

No one can take my stories from me. No one can tell them like I can. I want to do it with kindness, humor, and regard for the listener. I want to do it with power, boldness, and the authority of the Holy Spirit. You have stories to tell. Someone is waiting to hear them.

Your Thoughts?

_____

_____

_____

_____

_____

_____

_____

_____

_____

_____

_____

_____

_____

_____§

14~ Do You See Me?

It was an ordinary day. They carried the lame beggar to his usual place at the Temple gate called Beautiful. He knew no other life. Having been lame since birth, he had never walked or run with purpose and joy. He had no expectations. His head was low, not making eye contact. His demeanor was one of defeat and humiliation. He had no hope of a different life. 'Here comes two men who hung around Jesus of Nazareth', he may have thought to himself. 'What will they do for me?' He did what he always did; with downcast eyes he waited. Unexpectedly, his life was to change. Looking straight into his eyes, Peter said with authority, *"Look at us!"* The beggar lifted his head and looked right at them expecting money. 'We have no money to give you, but we will give what we have! *"In the name of Jesus of Nazareth, stand and walk."'* Reaching in faith with his right hand, Peter grasped the beggar's arm and helped him to stand. Suddenly, healing power was pouring into his ankles and feet. The next minute he was walking around and leaping with joy, shouting praises to God. People noticed. A crowd gathered. For Peter, it was another opportunity to speak of Jesus Christ and urge others to repentance and faith. For the beggar, he knew that God had seen him. These men who had been with Jesus, and were filled with the Holy Spirit, brought something to him that the beggar had never known; presence, dignity, and restoration (Acts 3).

Consider This: How often do we rise in the morning to follow our routine? We have stopped expecting the unexpected. I want to arise each morning with a sense of expectation and excitement to meet the power of Heaven in a new fresh way. I want to say *"I will arise in the light of the Lord!"* (Micah 7). This is how we are to live; filled with wonderment that the One who sees us loves us. He came from Heaven to give us hope. Each morning we can walk in faith, knowing that anything is possible with Him who never leaves us or forsakes us. The healed man, who sat outside the gate called Beautiful most of his life, learned this truth. He could say in his heart that *"He has made everything beautiful in its time"* (Ecclesiastes 3). Hagar, the maidservant, learned this when God came and spoke precious promises to her in a dark time. *"She gave this name to the*

29

LORD who spoke to her, 'You are the God who sees me,' for she said, 'I have now seen the One who sees me.'" (Genesis 16).

Did you know that the Greek word for Beautiful used in Acts 3 roughly means flourishing in the right hour or season? The lame man sat at a gate that declared his life held promise, even though he could not see it. The gate between the old and new way of life is Jesus Christ. Your life holds such unimaginable promise! Will you lift your head in His presence and receive, with dignity and joy, your heritage in Jesus?

Your Thoughts?

_____

_____

_____

_____

_____

_____

_____

_____

_____

_____

_____ §

_____

15~ A Courageous Life

Once again drama is unfolding. People crowded around the familiar lame man to see him walk and leap, praising God. Peter and John proclaimed Jesus Christ to those listening. They asked 'Why does this miracle surprise you?' It was clamorous and maybe unruly. Some people were not happy for this miracle. They could not rejoice over God's goodness in healing this man. It was something they could neither explain nor control. The religious leaders threw Peter and John in prison overnight to question them. For Peter and John, it was just another wonderful opportunity to tell of Jesus. The number of believers increased. But people knew Peter and John had been with Jesus. With cease-and-desist orders issued, they left the prison. Seeking other believers, they prayed, *"Now, Lord, consider their threats and enable your servants to speak your word with great boldness. Stretch out your hand to heal and perform signs and wonders through the name of your holy servant Jesus."* The room shook. The Holy Spirit filled many more people. They boldly spoke the Word of God. The apostles continued to testify of Jesus. God's great grace was on them. Their message was always the same straightforward truth of who Jesus is, who we are and God's plan from the beginning for a Savior. They were courageous, bold, filled with great power, and great grace. (Acts 4).

Consider This: My desire is for Courage, Boldness, Great Power and Great Grace. These were the men and women who had locked themselves in a room a short while before. The Holy Spirit transformed them. They knew the Holy Spirit came to impart authority to the proclaimers. It is God's purpose and timing to draw us with grace, impart faith to believe and the power to heal. We never know when God will disrupt natural physical laws in a holy display of the miraculous.

I will pray as these courageous men and women did. If ordinary people could ask and receive the Holy Spirit, I can too. I know I have this treasure in me. The great power I have in me is from God, given by grace (2 Corinthians 4).

Your Thoughts?

31

_____

_____

_____

_____

_____

_____

_____

_____

_____

_____

_____

_____

_____

_____

_____

_____

_____

_____

_____§

16~ Holy Interception

Peter had said to the lame man, *"I have no money but what I do have I give you in the name of Jesus Christ."* (Acts 3). This is an example of interception, as opposed to intercession. To intercept means to obstruct in a way that prevents someone from continuing to a destination. In the above case, Peter's interception prevented the lame man from continuing in lameness, life limitations, begging and unbelief. To intercede means to plead or petition on behalf of someone in difficulty or trouble. God calls us to intercede on behalf of others according to His heart. In the spiritual sense, interception and intercession are two different yet powerful holy acts of intervention. Jesus Christ is the divine interceptor and intercessor. He has intercepted my life by responding to my sin with His forgiveness and my doubt with assurance. Spiritual order replaced disorder. Peace replaced anxiety. Clarity replaced confusion. Abundance replaced lack. Love dispelled loneliness. Fortitude and victory overtook fear. It changed the course of my life. It is His life for mine with all the spiritual benefits and responsibilities of a life in right alignment with God by faith in the death and resurrection of Jesus Christ.

<u>Consider This:</u> You and I are to follow in His steps. I can learn to be an interceptor by studying His life: to offer others what I can give in Jesus' name. Not by retaliating in the same manner. He has equipped me, by the Holy Spirit, to intercept unlovely behavior with His grace, hate with His love, wrongs against me with forgiveness, anger with peace so they may know Jesus. Intercession is a private matter between God and me on behalf of others. Interception is harder for me as it is a public offering with the risk of getting it wrong. I must trust the Holy Spirit to guide and teach me.

Considering today's reflection, I am grateful for everyone who has ever offered me interception in Jesus' name. I would not be in relationship with Him today without it.

Your Thoughts?

§

17~ The Voice in the Fire

While Moses was on the top of Mount Sinai talking to God and receiving the ten commandments, the rest of the Israelites were waiting at the foot of the mountain. God spoke out of the fire, the cloud and thick gloom with a great voice. When they heard Him, they said *"we have heard His voice from the midst of the fire; we have seen this day that God speaks with man."* They were eager to hear the words of God but they asked Moses to go talk to Him. They were afraid they would die in His presence. Moses stood between them and God. God spoke in a great voice; His heart for the people (Deuteronomy 5).

Consider This: Shavuot, the Jewish holiday to commemorate the day God gave the Torah at Mount Sinai, set me thinking about God speaking from the midst of the fire. I love God's heart shown to me by scripture and the Holy Spirit. He wants a relationship with me (and you), whom He has always loved. The giving of the Torah was a gift from His heart of loving kindness. The Law shows us how impossible it is to live a perfect life. Its purpose is to draw people to God through Jesus Christ who paid the penalty for our sin and rose again to give us new life in Him. Jesus stands between us and God as Moses did with the Israelites.

When I go through a 'fire' in my life, it burns and sears my soul. I can forget for a while that God speaks from the midst of the fire. The same goes for those dark gloomy places I experience. He persists until I hear. He does not walk away in disgust because I did not listen the first or second time. He uses this time to draw me near. He prepares my heart to hear. He persistently speaks and is with me.

It is the voice of a Father. I can sense His heart beat quicken when I invite Him to speak again. He says, *"I have loved you with an everlasting love; I have drawn you with unfailing kindness,"* (Jeremiah 31). He says, *"For I know the plans I have for you"*, declares the Lord, *"plans to prosper you and not to harm you, plans to give you hope and a future."* (Jeremiah 29). I am grateful that scripture reminds me that *"He will be the sure foundation for your times, a rich store of salvation, wisdom and*

35

knowledge; the fear (awe, respect) of the Lord is the key to this treasure.' (Isaiah 33).

The Holy Spirit speaks so we may know our Father in heaven. Our Abba, Daddy. He is speaking. Keep listening. You will hear. He will make sure you do. I am praying for you.

Your Thoughts?

_____

_____

_____

_____

_____

_____

_____

_____

_____

_____

_____

_____

_____

_____

_____ §

18~ Love That Surpasses Knowledge

How can we grasp how wide, long, high, and deep the love of Christ is for us? It is a love that surpasses knowledge. Love is irrational in the sense we do not love with our minds but our hearts. We yearn to know without a doubt that God loves us. People live with despair without knowing. When we know God loves us, we can be strong. He loves us beyond our total comprehension. Circumstances and people cannot disrupt our identity in Christ's love.

Consider This: I am convinced that many people have a hard time knowing God's love for them, because the rationalism of our culture gets in the way. Or we believe what others have said to us with unkind words. Our minds get in the way. We want His love to ease our emotional pain rooted in the belief we are not lovable. With our minds, we try to rationalize God's love into human terms. I believe that God's love comes by revelation to the spirit of man.

At some point, I realized that my identity in Christ's love needed to be stronger. My spirit was not lighted as a *"lamp of the LORD."* (Proverbs 20). I began my search for this treasure by asking Him for it. I invited Him into places I had never thought to ask Him. In my searching, He came to me in a personal full-on experience of the Love He is. Love pulsed and radiated from Him as an unstoppable force. It flowed over and through me as mighty waves of warm healing balm. It was not a physical experience but of my spirit. He was lighting up my spirit with His love. It was healing at the deepest level. I have a knowing deep within me. My Father in heaven honored my search and met my greatest need. I now have an unshakeable identity in Him. This is one of the amazing functions of our spirits; to receive God. God loves you. He waits for you to seek Him. Will you?

Your Thoughts?

§

19~ Show Us the Father

Have you ever had a deep longing to know God as Father; as a nurturing parent? I have. The disciple Philip did. In a poignant exchange, Philip took advantage of the fact that Jesus welcomed questions. Being approachable, He treated their questions with respect and honesty. John 14 records the exchange. Philip said, *"Lord, show us the Father and that will be enough for us."* Jesus answered, *"Anyone who has seen me has seen the Father."* He wants us to ask Him questions so He can teach us, exchange the lies we believe for truth; to heal our wounds and make us whole. He spent His entire earthly life in pursuit of showing us His Father. His teaching, action and love, signs, and wonders give us an understanding of His true nature; so different from the gods of this world.

Consider This: I became like Philip, asking Jesus to show me my spiritual Father in heaven. He honored my request and lead me to Psalm 103. *"The Lord is compassionate and gracious, slow to anger, abounding in love. He will not always accuse, nor will he harbor his anger forever; he does not treat us as our sins deserve or repay us according to our iniquities. As a father has compassion on his children, so the Lord has compassion on those who fear (respect) him."* He led me to 1 Corinthians 13. *"Love is patient, love is kind. It is not easily angered. It keeps no record of wrongs. It always protects, always trusts, always hopes, always perseveres. Love never fails."* This is God's own description of His heart in action toward us.

We can ask Him to show Himself as both father and mother; the one who gives life, watches over, preserves, and gives abundantly. He will teach us so we can say with the writer of Psalm 131 that we are content.

He wants to heal that which hinders us from knowing Him intimately. His love transforms and sets us on a firm foundation. May you say with me, we have not received a spirit of bondage again to fear, but we have received the Spirit of divine adoption as sons and daughters, to whom we cry Abba! Daddy! Father! (Romans 8).

Your Thoughts?

_____

_____

_____

_____

_____

_____

_____

_____

_____

_____

_____

_____

_____

_____

_____

_____ §

20~ Abandoned by God? Never!

An abandoned person can feel unwanted, not worth the trouble, unsafe, frightened, distrustful, and filled with pain they try to hide. They can develop an orphan heart. I believe an orphan spirit is working hard in the world to convince us we do not belong, especially that God will not be careful with our hearts. It serves to keep us from our full identity as sons and daughters of God.

A person with an orphan heart does not know God as father or His mothering heart. An orphan heart may give up and deny the need for anyone. We believe we are on our own. We may pursue careers and relationships that give us what we lack in identity. The orphan heart can become anxious and controlling. It can create a sense of loneliness, abandonment, insecurity, and alienation. Performance for acceptance, self-medicating, isolation, or over-compensating become means of coping. It can push others away by expressing pain in fits of rage or self-criticism. All the time we have spent energy compensating for the lack, we have a spiritual Father who loves us. But we cannot believe this good news.

How do you recognize someone with an orphan heart? It is very hard because most of us have become adept at hiding the shame in inventive ways, even from ourselves.

Consider This: The answer to an orphan heart is the Father's love. We break the power of the lie by knowing we are sons and daughters of God (Romans 8). He is a father to the fatherless and to those living without His love. He will not leave us alone. A good place to start is by asking Him to show Himself to us as a father. Search the scriptures for revelation of God the Father, who Jesus came to show us. Renounce the orphan spirit as a lie. Believe and take Him at His word. Keep leaning into Him with unveiled hearts until we let our souls fill to overflowing with His love. Seek other trustworthy people to help us; those who have already found their way into the Father's embrace. Beloved, He is worth knowing. Your heart can trust Him in every way. He is calling your name.

Your Thoughts?

_____

_____

_____

_____

_____

_____

_____

_____

_____

_____

_____

_____

_____

_____§

21~ I've Got a River of Life

Think about hope. Hope is an optimistic state of mind based on expectations of a positive outcome (or circumstances). Hope's opposites are dejection, hopelessness, and despair. Optimism describes a hope dependent on the state of our affairs, wishes or the vagaries of our emotional state. Hope, based on God's promises, is alive in Jesus alone and rooted in the faithfulness of God. When mixed with faith it produces strength and endurance. When we find ourselves in a low place, we can encourage ourselves by saying *"Why, my soul, are you downcast? Why so disturbed within me? Put your hope in God, for I will yet praise Him, my Savior and my God."* (Psalm 42). We have the inner power to persevere.

Consider This: Head waters of rivers are small as they trickle out of the ground. They can carve large river beds by their persistent forward movement. A river gets to where it is going, even if it must go underground for a while and bubble up somewhere farther along its path. Free-flowing rivers move anything that yields to them. The water sings as it moves over and around obstacles. You know when a river is alive and moving.

Real hope is like a spiritual river. The head waters of hope, may start as a trickle and become a powerful torrent, carving a deep path through our soul. It speaks, compelling us to leave behind the things that keep us stuck. Real hope can disentangle us by its sheer force. We must surrender to its flow. It can seem as if our hope disappears. He will hold on to us and hope will bubble up again. This is the difference between optimism and real living hope. We need to listen for hope so we recognize it when we hear it singing. Most Christians can quote Jeremiah 29:11. *"For I know the plans I have for you, declares the Lord, plans to prosper you and not to harm you, plans to give you hope and a future."* This is a go-to verse for many without realizing that verse 11 is a bridge verse to bring about the action in verses 12-13. *"Then you will call on me and come and pray to me, and I will listen to you. You will seek me and find me when you seek me with all your heart."* Our river of hope flows through a personal relationship with Christ. Seeking Him is our primary life purpose; the source of our hope. His presence reminds us that whoever puts their trust in Him will have rivers of living waters flowing from them (John 7) and the song of their soul begins again. *"Let us hold unswervingly to the hope we profess, for He who promised is faithful."* (Hebrews 10).

Your Thoughts?

_____

_____

_____

_____

_____

_____

_____

_____

_____

_____

_____

_____

_____

_____§

22~ Faith Fueled Hope

"*For what is our hope, or joy or the crown in which we will glory in the presence of our Lord Jesus when He comes? Is it not you?*" (1 Thessalonians 2). This verse is from one of Paul's letters to the church. Paul says his hope is you (and me) standing someday in the presence of Jesus Christ. This is my hope and joy!

<u>Consider This:</u> Real hope does not standalone. It does not exist without faith. Faith is the fuel for my hope that burns bright and steady, regardless of circumstances. Faith in Christ is the substance and evidence for my hope. It is my confident assurance about what I do not see (Hebrews 11). The Bible instructs me to always be prepared to give a gentle, respectful answer to everyone who asks me the reason for my hope, keeping a clear conscience (1 Peter 3).

We think of evidence as concrete, irrefutable proof of the existence of something or an action having taken place. A court of law will not accept hearsay evidence. A valid eyewitness account based on the trustworthy character of the witness is acceptable. The evidence of my faith is the trustworthiness of my Savior, Jesus Christ, who is the same yesterday, today and forever. It relies on what I read in the Bible inspired by the Holy Spirit and what He speaks to me. The Holy Spirit bears witness to Jesus' nature and His ability to redeem my life for heaven (Romans 8). These are what enable me to have and act in faith on His promises. Faith for which I cannot even take the credit. I do not base my belief on my human decision to believe by reasoning. It is a gift of grace from God (Ephesians 2). Every time I try to reason out my faith in human terms, I cannot do it. It does not seem possible. Yet, it is.

My hope comes from an eyewitness account of a changed life through faith in Jesus Christ. My own changed life is the evidence of my faith and current hope of being in His presence forever. When I focus on this, everything else pales in comparison. In the meantime, I have His promises. He loves me through everything in this life. I am holding fast to the confession of my faith without wavering, for He who promised is

45

faithful (Hebrews 10). I fix my eyes on Jesus, who is the perfecter of my faith (Hebrews 12), or I stumble.

Your Thoughts?

_____

_____

_____

_____

_____

_____

_____

_____

_____

_____

_____

_____

_____

_____§

23~ Awe Filled Approach

I awoke this morning with a worship song. It was there in my heart unbidden. It reminded me that the curtain, to the holy of holies in the temple, tore when Jesus died on the cross (Matthew 27). It signified that through Jesus' sacrifice, God gave access to people who desired to know Him. God no longer hid himself allowing only the High Priest to make intercession for people. Jesus died to make us holy by taking our sins on Himself. He came for an unholy people to have access to a holy God. How can we reconcile knowing God is approachable with the full sensibility of His holiness?

Consider This: Before I knew God was approachable, I was fearful of His judgement, rejection, and retaliation. After I knew, I realized that I had not always given Him the proper deference His holiness deserves. Jesus was so approachable during His earthly ministry he allowed great crowds of people to press in around Him and touch Him. He allowed children to sit on His lap as they clamored for His attention. His demeanor and tone of voice, although authoritative, drew people to Him. No one fell on their faces before Him. There were, however, many healings and inner transformations. After His resurrection, His followers rushed to touch Him in affection. He is relational, welcoming, and compassionate.

We read that *"the Son is the radiance of God's Glory."* (Hebrews 1). When the soldiers came to arrest Him before His crucifixion, He said *"I am He"* and they fell to the ground unable to stand (John 18). The innate power was in Him from the Father (I AM). Jesus submitted Himself to this act of love on our behalf. He was arrested, tried, and crucified. At this moment the holiness of God overcame the soldiers. They could not remain upright before Him when He identified Himself. Jesus is the Way or path for our desired relationship with a holy God. He admonishes, forgives our sin, provides, cares, heals, protects, and teaches us. He listens when we talk to Him and speaks His heart to us when we ask. We never need to be alone. He wants us to know Him. He has a plan to prosper us.

He will not harm us (Jeremiah 29). He shares His holiness with us, diminishing none of His own.

I can draw close to Him with an overwhelming reverence, admiration, respect, and with the confidence of a well-loved child. I am in awe of our personal, approachable Savior who shines with a bright glory to which even the sun cannot compare.

Your Thoughts?

_____

_____

_____

_____

_____

_____

_____

_____

_____

_____

_____

_____§

24~ Whispers

"Speak Lord, for your servant is listening." (1 Samuel 3). I try to listen daily. I ask 'What is on Your heart, Lord? What do you want to tell me?' Then I listen for His answer. I cannot always hear. It is because He is whispering. I lean in to hear. Whispering sounds are just a gentle breath not strong enough to engage our vocal cords. Whispers are hard to hear.

Try this: just breathe, exhaling loud enough for a soft sound, with your hand near your mouth. Exhale while slowly whispering 'I love you' the same way. Pay attention to how your breath sounds and feels. Do this softly with barely a sound, then louder and louder, still as a whisper. You can even whisper while inhaling. Could you feel each word distinctly on your hand? Each whispered word has its own power and impact.

Consider This: Our spirits have ears too, in a manner of speaking. We can hear things breathed into our spirits by the Holy Spirit. We have assurance that whatever He says will not be contrary to scripture. We can check what we think we have heard to make sure it is from Him and not our own desires or thoughts. While we are there, we can examine our hearts. Then ask forgiveness for any unrighteous thing that is hindering our communication and check to see if we have engaged in selective hearing. We may have to train our ears to recognize the voice of the Holy Spirit.

God whispers to draw me so close I can feel His breath on me, spiritually. He will just breathe on me at first so I know He is near and have His attention. He breathes creative life-filled breath for the spiritual planting and harvesting of new things. It brings warmth and moisture to grow the truth He speaks into me. I want to feel the power of each word.

I gather His words, as precious jewels, into the treasury of my spirit. In them, I find salvation, wisdom, and knowledge. I find courage, boldness, joy, forgiveness, freedom, and the other good things He provides on the feasting table before my enemies (Psalm 23). Here is a whisper from the Lord: *"Forget the former things; do not dwell on the*

49

past. See, I am doing a new thing! Now it springs up; do you not perceive it? I am making a way in the wilderness and streams in the wasteland." (Isaiah 43). Lord, breathe on me.

Your Thoughts?

_____

_____

_____

_____

_____

_____

_____

_____

_____

_____

_____

_____

_____

_____

_____ §

25~ You Matter to God

"Lord, you know everything there is to know about me. You perceive every movement of my heart and soul, and you understand my every thought before it even enters my mind. You are so intimately aware of me, Lord. You read my heart like an open book. You know every step I will take before my journey even begins. You've gone into my future to prepare the way, and in kindness you follow behind me to spare me from the harm of my past. With your hand of love on my life, you impart a blessing to me. This is just too wonderful, deep, and incomprehensible! Your understanding of me brings me wonder and strength. You formed my innermost being. Everything you do is marvelously breathtaking. How thoroughly you know me, Lord! You saw who you created me to be before I became me! Every single moment you are thinking of me! How precious and wonderful to consider that you cherish me constantly in your every thought! God, I invite your searching gaze into my heart. Examine me through and through; find out every hidden thing within me. Put me to the test and sift through all my anxious cares. See if there is any path of pain I'm walking on, and lead me back to your glorious, everlasting ways; the path that brings me back to you." Excerpt from Psalm 139 (TPT)

<u>Consider This:</u>   How can anything compare to the wonderful knowledge that God thought about you even before your conception? He first decided how you were to fit into His overall plan and He wrote it in a book in Heaven! You are custom designed and created so you can respond to Him and live life in His power. And He left His imprint on you. Think of how artists mark their works (with their signature or maker's mark) so that even years later we can know who created them. That is what God did with you. Human beings are distinct from God's other creatures in that we have the God given-ability to respond to our Creator. That is one of His special purposes for us.

Creating you was not enough! He goes even farther than that. He says *"See, I have engraved you on the palms of my hands."* (Isaiah 49). He tattooed you on His nail pierced palms. How often do you look at your hands? Far more than you realize. With your name on God's hands, He cannot forget you. He designed, created, breathed life into you at the right time in history. For such a time as this! Go now and be strong in His Name!

Your Thoughts?

_____

_____

_____

_____

_____

_____

_____

_____

_____

_____

_____

_____

_____

_____§

26~ No Regrets

I woke up today this side of Heaven. I know the Lord has appointed me for this day. It is wide open to His possibilities. Today is a new day of discovery of what He planned back when He knew all my days before He formed me. I suppose I could ignore this wonderful gift to spend it looking at yesterday; analyzing what I did not do so well and regretting the times I fell far short of His glory. But not anymore. If nothing outwardly changes around me today, I still have a rich inner life with Him that helps me to transcend my past and circumstances. I am thankful He has allowed my regrets to draw me to Himself. I want to live a life aware of His presence, acceptance, and a better way. This awareness is so important. I know He never leaves me. I can have unbroken communication with Him. A few days ago, I asked Him what He wanted to say to me. The exchange went something like this:

'My children do not know Who I am,' He said. 'Who, me?' I replied in surprise. 'Yes.' He answered. 'I am your Redeemer. This is what I do. I redeem people who come to me in faith. You forget sometimes. I have seen you picking up the weight of regret again. Beloved, I have redeemed your regrets!' 'Lord!' I exclaimed, followed by silence as I let this sink in, 'How do I stop this?' He replied tenderly, 'Child, give these memories to me. Every time regret shows up, remember with thanksgiving what I remember; that I have given you today and a future; a new purpose in Christ. I paid the price once. It was enough.'

Consider This: Have you ever tried to turn your head around 180 degrees to look behind you? Why not try it now? I just tried. I cannot do it without turning my body in the direction I want to face. It makes it difficult to walk forward into my future while trying to look behind me. My feet are trying to go forward but the rest of me is trying to go backwards. I am at a standstill, unless I want to stumble.

There is a time for regrets. It is when I first learn and accept that God has a better way for me in Jesus Christ. This is the time to grieve for what was, could have been and will never be. I am before the cross, giving

Him my sorrow, letting Him lift the pain from me and call me into newness of life in Him. He gives me beauty for the ashes I have brought Him. This is a picture of healthy regret. I grieve, repent, learn, let go, rejoice, and move on in Him.

When I find it hard to let go of the past, I am grateful God is patient with me. His desire is for an intimate relationship that includes two-way conversations which leaves the way open for me to approach Him. I remember the cross of Jesus where I can go often to rise in freedom following His path, letting go, knowing I am not alone in this thing. Regretting causes heart trouble (Genesis 6). *"The Lord regretted ... and His heart was deeply troubled."* Thank God, it did not end there. His unstoppable love made a way to fix His troubled heart and mine.

Incomplete regret takes me backward and keeps me stuck there. It reflects a misunderstanding or a forgetting of what happened for me at the cross and empty tomb. The tendency to focus on the past leads me back to guilt, shame, disappointment, and self judgement. It leaves me in a perpetual state of deep sadness. When I turn to look behind in regret, I might slip into unbelief again.

He will show me the ways I can seek to repair what I have done, if possible. I can never redeem myself. He did it for me. I accept there may be consequences but no condemnation to a life of bitter regretting (Romans 8). I know that even in these things God works it together for my good. He restores me to Himself and He sets my feet firmly on a new path through difficult situations. I can choose new ways of living that propel me forward. When my focus is forward, I remember the whole point of this life.

Every time the past sneaks up to steal my joy, I will turn away to say thank you to the One who loves me best. I can wake up to a new day and live it facing forward, forgetting the things which He has forgotten (Philippians 3). I turn my face toward my future in Jesus Christ (Isaiah 43). Will you come walk with me?

Your Thoughts?

_____

_____

_____

_____

_____

_____

_____

_____

_____

_____

_____

_____

_____

_____

_____

_____§

27~ The Sweet and The Savory

The apostle Mark said *"Salt is good, but if it loses its saltiness, how can you make it salty again? Have salt among yourselves and be at peace with each other."* (Mark 9). King David wrote that God's words were sweeter than honey. He prophesied the gall (bitter) given to Jesus on the cross; vinegar (sour) for His thirst. It is the sweet, savory, sour and bitter.

Consider This: Food is a timeless, universal metaphor. When our life is dull, we lack the savor of more exciting or interesting times. Sweet times are pleasant. Hard times are bitter.

A while back, I craved sweet foods, until I realized I had gotten somewhat off balance. Sweet things are easily available and are pleasant on my tongue but never fill me up or feed my body with what it needs. My energy was low and my brain was foggy. The path back to healthy eating started with the determination to prepare vegetables ahead of time and choose fruits for their sweetness. I started to feel better; the cravings ebbed. This experience reminds me of Paul's teaching in Hebrews 5-6, where he yearns to teach believers the meatier truths of God. Their continued desire for elementary spiritual truths frustrated him. They wanted what was available and easy to digest; to feed on foundational truths without building on them.

God speaks to us with sweet and hard words. When we get a helping of the bitter or sour things of life, He knows how to keep our faith strong and one foot in front of the other. We may feel beat up by life, unable to handle the more difficult deeper spiritual things. It can become a habit that lingers when our life eases and evens out. It is a natural thing to want to feast on words that sooth, encourage, build us up, and give us hope. The sweet milk of the Word is good.

There comes a time when we realize that if we are to grow in the Lord, we must be open to the deeper things. How else will our spiritual bones become strong enough to support a growing faith and trust in Him? How else will we have the spiritual vigor to walk our path with Him? Our sight needs to be keen and our hearing sharp to discern danger to our souls. Our spiritual reflexes must be able to react to enemy attacks. We need to build on the foundational truths that served us well as new believers. Otherwise, we will miss the ever-increasing glory of God to transform us to stand strong in battle strategy and to help others grow.

If I feast only on the easier things of scripture, how will I ever grow in my faith in Him? I cannot trust in His promises because I have never let Him take me out on a limb or into deeper waters. If I shrink back from exercising my spiritual muscles with the heavy lifting, I will stay weak. The giants will overcome and I will fall.

To counteract this natural tendency, I read my Bible and engage in bible studies to meditate on His deeper truths. I avail myself of the counsel and wisdom of more mature Christians, where I see the life of Christ formed more than in me. I try to align myself with the instructions to persevere in the trial. Perseverance must finish its work so I may be mature and complete (James 1). I ask for wisdom to understand the more mature aspects of being a believer in Christ and add those things to my foundational faith. These are the ways I eat my spiritual meat, vegetables, and fruits. I enjoy the sweet things in balance with the other good things of the Bible. I want to be salty in living my life in full view of the world so that others may want the savory things of God. With the bitter and the sour, I lean into Him more than ever for what only He can give me.

Where, you ask, does umami fit into the mix? I describe spiritual umami as that which I sense in my spirit but cannot explain. It is the uniqueness of communication that the Father allows while holding back the mystery I cannot yet fathom. His spirit speaks to mine, with unspoken words. Spiritual umami enhances the other flavors of my life in Christ that keeps me coming back for more and guards me until the day of His return. Come share a meal at His table with me.

Your Thoughts?

§

28~ Pray or Prey

Abram, the patriarch (later renamed Abraham), was living peacefully among allies in the land to which God had led him. There was a great war which led to the capture of his nephew Lot. Abram gathered his men and recovered Lot and his possessions. The king of Salem blessed him saying, *"Blessed be Abram by God Most High ... and praise be to God, who delivered your enemies into your hand."* After this, the king of Sodom demanded that he give Lot and his family to Sodom but to keep their possessions. Abram declined. He had vowed to take nothing from his enemies. The Lord encouraged him not to be afraid because He was Abram's shield. While he had God's attention, Abram brought up his promised heir who had not yet come. The Lord reassured him. That was when the birds of prey came to steal his worship (his sacrifice) and Abram shooed them away. It was after this that God affirmed His promises for Abram's two most important desires: an heir and a place to belong (Genesis 14-15).

Consider This: The order of these events has great relevance for us today. Abram believed God and left his old life. He began the new life God gave him. This new land had enemies who tried to take from Abram. He was bold and victorious in battle. His enemies tried to undermine him. God affirmed His promises. Abram believed. When birds of prey came to steal his worship, Abram shooed them away. God delivered His promises.

I am thinking about the birds of prey. Birds of prey are predatory by nature. They have hooked bills and sharp talons to grab their prey on the fly. They are aggressive and unrestrained in attack. The second thing that impressed me was that Abram stayed with God, not engaging with his enemies.

I have a choice: I can pray or be prey. As a believer, I live a life of great promise. The promises of God are many. I live in a world where my spiritual enemy is as a bird of prey who comes to devour my identity in Christ; to steal my faith and joy in God. No believer is exempt from these aggressive assaults. I have mountain top experiences where I am courageous, go to battle and win. It is when I least expect it, when I am tired and not alert, that I am most susceptible to becoming prey. The enemy of my soul swoops in and tries to grab the things that matter most to me. He attacks my spiritual identity and the promises God has given me. I am easy-pickings. I give in and speak aloud from this tired place agreeing with the enemy. Until I remember, that the Lord always makes a way of escape. I can run to Him for cover and protection. He is my deliverer from the trap. I can talk to the One who loves me best and encourage myself in Him. I can speak aloud His promises and wave away the spiritual birds of prey and continue to worship. My strength comes from Him.

Your Thoughts?

§

29~ Winning the Game

Abandoned, betrayed, forgotten, falsely accused, and imprisoned. Born a favored son of a large family, through a series of misfortunes, young Joseph began a new life as a slave. It began with the treacherous actions of his brothers. The rest of his life was mostly out of his control. He wanted love, respect, protection, and affirmation. I imagine he experienced fear and despair when his happy world went wrong, wondering why God had allowed this path. But his story, starting in Genesis 30, mentions nothing. Joseph's story portrays his choices in the face of unfair circumstances and how God moved powerfully through them. It is a story of Joseph's intentional relationship and reliance on God. He trusted God in the difficulties he faced. He responded in faith to one sad thing after another. He said at the family reunion, *"it was not you who sent me here, but God."* (Genesis 45). It is an amazing story and one worth reading again.

Consider This: Joseph did not make his choices because he knew the results in advance. He chose with integrity and steadfastness. Along the way, Joseph reconciled his life with God and forgave his brothers, putting away bitterness and resentment. Do you think this transformation occurred in a pit in a wild country or as a slave in the desert? Did he have an epiphany as the highest trusted steward in a ruler's household, forgotten in prison, or as the second most powerful man in Egypt? Yes, it happened in all these places. He lived without knowing why until God showed how the events fit together, when he and his brothers looked into each other's eyes again. It had been so he could protect and preserve his family, who were God's promise to Abraham. This is the moment he showed great emotion as he privately wept.

I have often considered Joseph's choices. I learn many things from him. I am grateful that I am a child of God in Christ Jesus because of this man's faith. God preserved Joseph for a purpose. Joseph yielded. He humbled himself and learned to dwell in the secret place of God (Psalm 91). He lived there, loved. God knows where you are in life. He loves you and is speaking His purposes over you. He knows tomorrow and the next day; your future. He is trustworthy. Keep talking and listening to Him! He has things to say that no one else can tell you. Let us stay in the game to win the race! Let us hold on to Whom we believe and trust Him with every aspect of our lives.

Your Thoughts?

_____

_____

_____

_____

_____

_____

_____

_____

_____

_____

_____

_____

_____

_____§

30~ When Hope Trumps Despair

Consider Hagar, Sarah's slave, introduced in Genesis 16. Sarah in desperation, gave Hagar to Abraham to produce an heir (a common practice in that culture). Hagar conceived and made the mistake of acting superior to Sarah. Sarah, resentful, made life unbearable for Hagar, who fled into the desert. In this unlikely place, the seed of hope took root in Hagar giving her strength. When she was alone and desperate God met her by a spring. He told her she would bear a son called Ishmael, which means 'God will hear', because He had heard her misery. She called the Lord who met her in her distress *"You are the One who sees me."* She gave the well she was resting by a new name, *"The well of the Living One who sees me."* A new thing started that day when hope defeated despair.

Have you noticed how many stories in the Bible tell of new beginnings? God created the Earth and all life on it. New dynasties began and people moved to new places. A Child was born, who was the Son of God, to bring peace between God and man. Renewed hearts and minds follow God to where ever He leads them.

The Lord is always doing something new in our lives. His mercies are new every morning! Each day offers new hope in Him. Unhappy places can contain seeds of hope when we trust our lives to God in Christ Jesus. I love the story of Hagar for its hope and restoration. I can look back on my life and remember the places where the Lord met me and renewed my trust in Him. He gave me hope to continue in difficult situations. He spoke in Isaiah 42, *"See, the former things have taken place, and new things I declare."* He showed me a better way to live my life with His love and direction leading me forward. He loved me enough to tell me good things were coming even though I could not see them. He accepted me into a place of belonging.

<u>Consider This:</u> Every time I find myself in new circumstances or moving in a different direction, I struggle with how to do this new thing? I have so many choices to make. Because of Hagar's story, I know He

will hear when I ask Him where to start and which path to take. I ask God, who sees me, to walk with me because He has been to my future and knows the way. I rely heavily on the fact He prepared in advance for me (Ephesians 2). I trust that He will show me the things I do not know (Jeremiah 33), as I walk into unfamiliar places. He will give the courage (Joshua 1). I begin by saying, 'Yes, Lord'. This is the moment new hope arrives.

Your Thoughts?

_____

_____

_____

_____

_____

_____

_____

_____

_____

_____

_____

_____§

31~ Living in Hope

A sad aspect of our times, many people do not thrive as God intended because they feel unwanted by others and God. Real hope, ignited by knowing Whose we are, is the way out of this isolating life. There is a spiritual hunger and seeking to belong to end the loneliness. The world offers us many paths which lead to temporal hope. We have a lot of choices.

Consider This: I write about eternal hope; the hope we can have in Christ Jesus. I remember a time when I did not have hope in Him. It was a painful place. Nobody goes through life unscathed by hardship and challenges. When we think we can go through life without suffering, we deceive ourselves. It can lead us to embrace anger and hopelessness. 'It is not fair!', we cry and focus on our lack by comparing our life with others.

The Bible uses the word hope 129 times with the meaning of *a confident expectation*, patience, and trust in God. I write about the heroes of faith in the Hebrews hall of fame (chapter 11) because they followed the light when they could not see it. They encourage me to do the same. These people were still living by faith when they died. It says that God was not ashamed of their representation of Him on earth. We have the example of Christ who understands our weakness because He lived in a human body as we do. He lives now to plead before the Father for us; to strengthen us to endure. How can this not give us hope?

There is a place in the brain that lights up when we are hopeful. A place right behind our eyes. It is interesting because if we see our desire, we no longer hope for it. Hope based on the promises of God, which we cannot see, is life-giving and infuses us with strength. With hope, we can live fruitful lives in the middle of hardship and challenges. There is nothing on earth that can give us the encouragement that spiritual hope in Jesus brings. He is a precious Treasure.

We have the power to live joyfully; steadfast in faith. We can look on those around us who are struggling and offer them hope with a generous spirit. We can ask God to help as we offer them what we can, because He is our Hope. I pray for us to turn to the One who can give a confident expectation and patience. He provides His kind company along the way as we offer this hope to others. Are you seeking deeper hope? Are you a hope carrier to others?

Your Thoughts?

_____

_____

_____

_____

_____

_____

_____

_____

_____

_____

_____

_____§

32~ When Seasons Change

As I write, the leaves are changing into vibrant autumn colors of red, gold, and yellow. We take rides to view this amazing display. Autumn leaf-peeping is a sensory experience. We seek trees in groups, splashing their complementary colors everywhere. We spy a magnificent tree standing alone, breathtaking in its splendor. We love to take hikes and smell the unique essence of fallen leaves as they crunch beneath our feet. We smell snow in the air and prepare for winter. In several months, we will look eagerly for the bright green leaves of spring.

Consider This: I can get comfortable in seasons of my life and when I sense that something is changing, it often takes a while to accept what is coming. As I get an inkling, I may dig in my heels to stop the advance. It will take time to let the Holy Spirit do His holy work to prepare me. Each season has a different preparation period and approach. The only constant is the Holy Spirit who lives within me and leads me through it. I have learned to rely on the promises from the Promise Maker who is the promise keeper (2 Peter 1). The Bible is full of promises from a loving Father. He moves within me to grow me into maturity in His truths. A favorite Bible verse is Isaiah 33, *"He will be the sure foundation for your times, a rich store of salvation and wisdom and knowledge; the fear of the LORD is the key to this treasure."* This verse holds me and I know I am secure in the transition.

Do you have one Bible verse you like better than the others, that speaks to you in every season and settles you? Your verses may change with each season of life. We can ask Him for the ones that will give us what we need at every moment. While we cannot stop the inevitable changes, we can lean into Him with assurance He never leaves us. I am speaking over my life from Psalm 139 (TPT-The Passion Translation). *"You know every step I will take before my journey even begins. You have gone into my future to prepare the way, and in kindness you follow behind me to spare me the harm of my past. With your hand of love on my life, you impart a blessing to me."* With this powerful declaration and God's affirmation, I can breathe in anticipation of new things to come. I hope you are declaring His promises over your life today.

Your Thoughts?

_____

_____

_____

_____

_____

_____

_____

_____

_____

_____

_____

_____

_____

_____§

33~ What is This Lord?

We learn from a young age to say the 'magic words' when making a request of another? 'Please' and 'thank you' are words of politeness to show respect to the person addressed. Every time I say please, I am asking for someone's favor. Most languages have a word or phrase for please — por favor (Spanish), s'il vous plaît (French) and prego (Italian). As children we learn the simple word 'please' gives us access to things we might otherwise not receive, hence the magic in them.

Consider This: The Lord's favor is righteousness when we confess our sin. Protection when buffeted on every side, rain in dry times, resources in scarcity, healing when ill and good things from His hand are the favor of the Lord. Do we sometimes look at the answer we have received from God's hand and wonder what He is thinking? What do we do with what He gave, when it is nothing like we wanted, even though we said please?

The northwestern islands of Scotland are complete with mountains, rocks and large stones strewn everywhere. It can be cold, with strong winds. These islands are breathtaking and inhospitable. Yet generation after generation have called this isolated land home for thousands of years. They learned the secret of living on these remote islands. They used whatever they found to improve their lives. They built homes and fences with thick walls of the plentiful stone for warmth and protection. They cooked their food and warmed their homes with peat from the earth. The natural resources of plentiful stones, rocks and dirt are an example of the Lord's favor in this environment.

When the Lord's favor comes in the form I do not expect, it may look like a hard, unyielding stone, a clod of dirt or a cold icy wind. I cry out 'Where are you God? What do I do with this?' He answers that he looks for those who are *"humble and contrite in spirit and tremble at His word."* (Isaiah 66). I am trembling when looking at the disguised favor. But do I have a humble and contrite heart? Here I am, on my knees again, asking to see what He intends for me to do with this favor He has given. Metaphorically will I be able to see it as raw material for cooperating with Him as He teaches me what to do with it? Will I see Him in these things He has favored me with in love? Will I see Him? Will I see? This is the cry of my heart; to know how close He is, to know His protection, strength, forgiveness, and compassion. I want to recognize and accept it in whatever form it comes.

Your Thoughts?

_____

_____

_____

_____

_____

_____

_____

_____

_____

_____

_____

_____

_____

_____§

34~ What is my Jericho?

The book of Joshua, in the Old Testament, is a fast-moving action filled story, depicting God moving on behalf of His people. It tells of an amazing victory activated by faith in His promises. It is full of precise God-given strategy to the Israelites as they prepared to take the land promised to them. This is a story overflowing with lessons that are still valid and powerful today.

The setting for the drama is a late bronze age city built on a high hill. I have read that the wall was a combination of different walls rising along the embankment. There were lower and upper city walls. The city wall (three cascading walls), as viewed on the ground, would have appeared to be ten stories high; approximately 70ft (21m). It would have appeared to be an impenetrable fortress to the average person. They were not a great army and had none of the usual tools of war for conquering even a tiny flat city. How was it they won a great victory which still captures interest today?

<u>Consider This:</u>   Israel's commander, Joshua, believed the promises God made to him and applied the directive to be strong and courageous. He lived his life as one who saw the possibilities. He saw the obstacles and challenges and still focused on God's powerful promises. He was a Philippians 4:13 guy. He sought God's perspective as he mulled over the challenges facing him. In response, God sent His heavenly commander to prepare Israel to receive strategy for this battle.

God's strategy was for them to sanctify themselves to Him, remember His promised deliverance and eat from the land as if it was already theirs. He told them to line up, move, move again, keep moving. Shout! I can hear Joshua saying 'Okay people, did you get that? Now *"consecrate yourselves, for tomorrow the Lord will do amazing things among you."* (Joshua 3). And they moved as one. There is archeological evidence of this battle, stone rubble and burnt wheat supplies in the place where Jericho once rose as a fortress.

I ask myself: What is my Jericho? What insurmountable challenge am I seeing? What strategy is God speaking to me? Will I live with a Philippians 4 focus? My better self says I will. Because faith moves God and God moves mountains. He tumbles walls. What is your Jericho today? How will you move? Will you declare you can do all this through Him who will give you strength? (Philippians 4:13).

Your Thoughts?

_____

_____

_____

_____

_____

_____

_____

_____

_____

_____

_____

_____

_____§

35~ God Does the Rest

The other day a runner's image at the starting block popped into my head. Since I am the least sports-oriented person I know, I knew the Holy Spirit had something for me to hear. I knew the purpose of running a race is for the fastest person to win by speed and perseverance over short or long distances. I have since learned that the starting position and the first action determines the smoothness of the entire race. Starting acceleration influences speed. Athletes practice setting up to get comfortable with each position. Movements and actions are precise to gain leverage and speed with good form; to outrun others. There is the need to build up supporting muscles and lung capacity for overall endurance. It is a science. It is serious business for those who want to win. Form, conditioning, and mental focus are factors in running well and finishing a race. Have you ever seen a reclining chair at the starting line? The race would be over before the runner stood. Have you ever seen a wishful runner? They are the ones who are still walking around warming up when the starting pistol sounds muttering, 'I wish I may, I wish I might...'. A successful race depends on preparation, positioning, readiness for action, and perseverance.

<u>Consider this:</u> Many ancient people of bible times can teach us a thing or two about preparation, readiness, and perseverance. Hebrews 11 is the powerful testimony of victorious runners whose accolades start with By Faith. Obedience, preparation, reaction time, spiritual muscle development, and perseverance with a God-centered focus, mark their legacy. They won their race and the purse at the end—a special deposit made into their spiritual bank account. They believed God and learned first-hand He is faithful. They had to lay aside every hindrance (or comfortable recliner chair), to run with endurance while looking to Jesus for what they lacked. We can have the same victory today when we align with Him. These people had stamina in their faith, they hoped for what they could not see and they lived very far from the old 17th century nursery rhyme that ends with 'If wishes and buts were candy and nuts, every day would be Christmas.' Encourage yourself and each other as we

run the race set before us. Dreams are good to have but when the wishing impedes running with endurance, we need to regroup. We can adjust our starting stance and our thoughts moment by moment to align with God's truth.

There is a secret to perseverance. Take one step at a time, then another and another. Some of our steps are small, hesitant, and short. Other steps are long, purposeful and gain ground. Each step matters in bringing us closer to the finish line. God's word lights our path and feet to keep us from stumbling. We do our best and God does the rest. Come, run with me for the joy set before us.

Your Thoughts?

_____

_____

_____

_____

_____

_____

_____

_____

_____

_____§

36~ Gold in the Sun

Have you ever asked God to explain things that have happened to you? Job did. He said, 'My complaint is legitimate. Where can I find God so I can state my case to Him? He will not rebuke me for asking. Even if I do not know where He is, He knows where I am. I will come out of this test as gold.' Job knew that while he may never understand all that God allows, he was confident that God knows what He is doing. He was steadfast when his friends and family told him to turn his back on his uncaring God and die. The Lord knows where I am in my journey. He allows me to come talk to Him. He speaks and I listen. Sometimes we go over the same stuff. The comforting part is that He sees me and knows where to find me. In the middle of whatever is happening, God is working it out for my good. He promised this in Romans 8.

<u>Consider this:</u> Gold powder is the purest form of gold. It is so light it can, under certain circumstances, weigh less than nothing. Exposing the powder to high heat turns it into a pure transparent glass-like substance with just a sheen of gold. Gold in its natural state is heavy and dense because of the impurities present in it. Most of the gold in the world has impurities. Pure gold has unique purposes as a perfect superconductor because nothing is there to hinder the transmission. There is an amazing story here of our worth. It is hard hearing this in the middle of the fire. I know because I have been in spiritually purifying fires. Through it, I have learned He has not forgotten me and I am a beloved child. He knows where to find me and come alongside. He allows me to lean in close and hear His heart beat as He speaks my name. Others have come through their fire and helped me on my way. For some earthly purposes, impurities are necessary in gold. But we have an eternal purpose. He means for us to reflect Him as gold shines in the sun; to be pure and transparent. We are to be superconductors of His presence.

I am writing today to remind us: God has not forgotten us. We are pearls of great price. He sent His Son Jesus to show us who He is, to take our impurities on Himself on the cross. When I need affirmation, it helps to remember He wants to take my stuff, turn it to gold and love me through the fire. When I come through it, I will shine like gold in the sun.

Your Thoughts?

_____

_____

_____

_____

_____

_____

_____

_____

_____

_____

_____

_____

_____§

37~ God-Sized Dreams

I remember hesitating as my finger paused over the Publish button for my first post in my 'Eyes to See Ears to Hear' blog. It was such a huge step for a private, introverted person. It had been a dream of mine to write. I was seconds away from starting, and I froze. Then, I remembered why I was doing it. During a retreat with friends, we heard the story of the Samaritan woman with the alabaster box of ointment. I heard the Holy Spirit say to me 'Identity' and a second later the speaker said 'The woman with the box had identity issues'. I heard the Holy Spirit say, 'Break it down, Shirley!' and immediately after that the speaker said, 'The woman had to break the box to get the precious out!'. It was a powerful moment. The Holy Spirit had my attention. If I wanted to write, I had to break through my private comfort level, insecurities, and fears; and trust Him. I had to be vulnerable. My finger hit Publish. I was on my way. He has given me much assurance of His plan for me. I ask Him to make His voice louder than any other so I can hear Him above the rest. I turn to Him to voice my insecurities. He has been faithful. I cannot tell the half of it here.

Consider This: When was the last time you thought about your own dreams; living your life experiencing His faithfulness as you follow what He has set before you to do? Have you started to live your dreams in alignment with His plans for you and with Him? Each of us has a God-size purpose for His timing. He has plans for us. God-sized dreams are bigger than our current abilities, require more resources than we have and take us to places we never thought to go and we do not know how to do. We need Him to show us step by step, trusting Him for resources, to open doors and present opportunities. We need to hear Him say "Now!" and then move in His light.

When we are not sure of our identity in Jesus, we can look at others for our own validation, affirmation and worth. We can sacrifice the purposes of our lives to live through others and live their dream instead of our own. Or we can just stall out and have none. Jesus wants to be the one who validates, affirms, and values us. Otherwise, our dreams will stay dreams. I hope you live your God-sized dreams that God-has given you. Someone is waiting for you to go for it.

Your Thoughts?

_____

_____

_____

_____

_____

_____

_____

_____

_____

_____

_____

_____

_____

_____§

38~ Moving the Marbles

I never know when the Holy Spirit will show up through everyday things. Friends re-introduced us to the childhood game of Chinese Checkers. It is most fun when the center gets all jammed up with each player using their own strategy to get to their goal. My strategy as an adult differs from when I was a child. I am more of an offensive player now. I move my marbles around to keep moving forward and get closer to my home goal, regardless of what the other players are doing. It is not about keeping other players in check to give me an advantage. It is so I can move past the other marbles in the most skillful and fastest way without spending too much effort on blocking. It takes strategic thinking and planning, even for this simple game. This is not only true in the games I play but in how I approach life. God has changed me. I live freer because I trust Him to show the way and provide for the journey. I do not spend as much time and energy worrying about the obstacles in my path. With Him by my side, I do my best to seek biblical strategies to win.

<u>Consider This:</u> Matthew 10 tells us to be on guard, shrewd as snakes and harmless as doves. He is not telling us to be naïve and allow others to take advantage of us or we of them. He is saying for us to make our decisions based on His direction and purposes for our lives. He tells us the Holy Spirit will be with us in the hardest places. His desire is that we focus on what He tells us to do and not worry about how others respond. His plan for us is to prosper as we seek His path.

Our job is to throw off the things that hinder and jam up our life. It puts me in mind of when I was a child. I spoke, thought, and reasoned as a child. I made life decisions from a child's perspective. There comes a time to put away childish things to live as mature men and women of God. Although, we need to remain child-like in faith which is desirable. Strategizing our next move is not focusing on perpetual analysis, fearing failure, doing what the crowd does or other life limiting things. We can ask Him to release His plans for us on earth as they are in heaven. We can take the step He shows us and stay there until He shows us the next. The in-between times, when we wait, is when many wonderful things happen for us in preparation for the next step. Practicing patience is one thing we can do that is shrewd and harmless. The Holy Spirit knows when to set up our next move. He keeps us going in the right direction. Our first strategic move is to ask Him to lead us.

Let us dare to pray God honoring prayers, beyond our current faith level. Prayers that take us forward beyond our wildest dreams. Let us be bold in our faith, unafraid to follow Jesus where He leads us into a rich life, not having to see the next step ahead of time. When was the last time we let Him work in our lives in ways that astounded us? His promise is exceedingly abundantly above all we can ask or imagine. I am on the move! Are you?

Your Thoughts?

_____

_____

_____

_____

_____

_____

_____

_____

_____

_____

_____§

39~ Hocus Focus

We have a cardinal's nest in the holly at the south corner of our porch with three spotted eggs. I spooked the mama when I dug up burning bush shoots and planted tomato seeds. Early in the mornings I watch mourning doves build nests in the arborvitae and listen to their gentle cooing. Bright yellow warblers are flitting around with sweet tunes. A pair of huge Canadian geese, who frequent the wetland next door, flew over my head yesterday as I walked the driveway to get the mail. Their large shadows startled me. 'Cover your head and duck!', my inner child yelled. Their focus is on fostering new life. When I work at slowing my pace, I find I experience more life-giving moments. Why is it so hard for me to do this while the rest of God's creatures can focus on important things in their lives with little effort? None of them have planners, calendars, or reminder alarms.

Consider This: Jesus knows how to focus. He says He does only what He sees His Father doing. He teaches us who God is by everything He did and the stories He tells in the Bible because He knows how to focus on the important things. Hebrews 12 encourages me to focus my eyes on Jesus. He is the pathway to life. When I slow down to enquire of the Holy Spirit, worship the Lord and converse with Him, I learn to apply His wisdom. I look to the written word, the Bible. I tune my ear to listen for His responses in my spirit. I can align my thoughts, beliefs, and actions to them. Life becomes more focused as I learn to still my mind and consider what is most important. When we are in a relationship with Him, we can see what Jesus is doing and we can hear the Holy Spirit clearer. I have a lot to learn about focusing my eyes. I will turn my ear to wisdom and apply my heart to understand. I will call out for insight as it says in Proverbs 2. I will quiet myself before Him as He fosters new life in me.

The Son of God came to give inner abundance; one characterized by an intimate personal life with Him based on the turning away from sin and receiving forgiveness. If you do not have a relationship with Him, will you seek Him today? The book of John is a good starting place.

Your Thoughts?

_____

_____

_____

_____

_____

_____

_____

_____

_____

_____

_____

_____

_____

_____

_____ §

40~ Until We Meet Again

My prayer is for us to know God in all our circumstances.

To discern His heart in the matters of today.

To follow the Holy Spirit's direction, from Whom we are seeking guidance and revelation.

May He meet us on the road that leads away from our true purpose and walk with us on the path to the destination of His choosing.

For those He has called to join with us on the way; to heed His call and keep divine appointments.

For our hearts to be full and our voices declare gratitude for the plans He has for our futures.

Thank you for reading *A Confident Expectation*. I hope you share your hope with others.

Blessings.

~About the Author~

Shirley Genovese is full of hope. Her desire is to inspire others to seek a deeper relationship with God and live a life where hope can grow. You will usually find her reading a book or painting. Otherwise, she is writing a book. In her spare time from creative pursuits, you may find her and her husband walking in the woods. Any woods will do.

Shirley is excited to present *A Confident Expectation* which is a selection of conversations with readers highlighting her path to a deeper hope in Jesus Christ. Like the sun trying to shine through a thick canopy of leaves in the forest, sometimes all it takes for the light to come blazing through is a slight shift of vision and perspective. She hopes that this book will be a hope carrier delivering a way for that shift to occur and let hope arise in readers.

Shirley earned a Bachelor's Degree from the University of New York at Buffalo in Business Administration. She is a retired accountant and business manager. Shirley lives with her husband in Upstate New York. She is an artist who paints with an eye for light which, for her, symbolizes hope alive in its infinite manifestations.

www.shirleyagenovese.com

CPSIA information can be obtained
at www.ICGtesting.com
Printed in the USA
FFHW021857240719
53860885-59553FF

9 781733 174008